Exodus

Also by Cadeyn McLellan

Journey to the Sun
The Primordial Mind

Copyright information

Quotations taken from;
- Attenborough, D. (2011). *Life Stories* (No. 11) [Podcast *Life Stories*]. BBC.
- *King James Bible*. (1973). Holman Bible Publishers. (Original work published 1611)

All works quoted are in the public domain.

Cover art by Stefano B. Edied by Michael Martin. Artist photo taken by Bek Stokes. Published and distributed through Ingram Spark.

Copyright © 2025 by Cadeyn McLellan. All rights reserved. No portion of this book may be reproduced in any form without written permission from the publisher or author, except as permitted by U.S. copyright law.

ISBN: 978-1-7640159-2-9 First Edition Hardback.

Volume 3: Exodus

For my long-suffering parents.

Introduction

As a reckless child, I was blessed to have faithful parents. Their patient forbearance and biblical foundations certainly reduced my prodigal son inclinations. This may seem hard to believe, given the grief I put them through in dire hospital stays and innumerable visits to the Principle. The parental balance of freedom and constraint must have been so hard to find.

This collection is about the faith they taught me. Hopefully these poems show that not everything they said to me was ignored.

Volume 3
Exodus

Volume 3: Exodus

Chapter 1: A City Built on Good Intentions
1. Pandæmonium — 2
2. The Death of Kama and Skanda — 12
3. The Babel Poet — 14
4. Tenochtitlan — 16
5. Poltergeists — 20
6. Día de los Muertos — 28
7. Truth Set Sail — 30

Chapter 2: Nurtured by Sweet Nature
8. Seasonal Meditations — 40
9. Wright Valley Seals — 50
10. Water Dragon — 52
11. Pan — 53
12. Es Vedra — 54

Chapter 3: Word becomes Flesh
13. Coelacanth — 64
14. Reflections on the Apostles Creed — 66
15. Poetry — 72
16. Satan and the Rock — 75
17. Under the Sun — 78
18. Coelacanth Revisited — 82

A City Built on Good Intentions

Pandæmonium
First Circle

I walk alone through neon-painted trees,
For solitude is best society.
As wondering through the sustaining night,
It seems so long since I saw harsh sunlight.
Yet choice is mine in Paradiso.
Somewhere in bars of night and old depots,
I walk as nameless king in purple suit,
Descending busy streets and garbage chutes,
Passing shops through the old acropolis,
And tabled in cafe Metropolis.
As coffee on the incense altar burns,
Ascending smoke, descending scents return,
As bankers chatter the economy
And poets musing modern prophecies.
They fill me with familiarity,
My friends are strangers in sincerity.
My breath, my choice, the butter on my knife,
Infusing perfumes of this real life.
An individual of modern hue,
Enlightenment inside the waiter queue.
My own circadian rhythm is free;
There's no divine algorithm on me.
No destination in the city sprawl,
I built Eden inside these city walls.

Pandæmonium
Second Circle

Continuing onwards down Charon way,
Where a museum stood of ancient days,
The antiques flicker in the glowing lights,
In all reserved eternal copyright.
A Coelacanth who once rose from the deep,
Extinct again now in these remnants keep.
Some men beside with stones of feathered bite,
Still argue if the dinosaurs took flight.
The shelving filled with relics of the earth,
The artefacts of man in death and birth.
Some child's clothing faded long to grey,
Beside them a decaying vertebra.
To whom these once belonged no plaque to see,
Perhaps so long ago were owned by me.
Familiar these ancient forms of old,
Displacing spectral forms of earthly hold.
A plastic doll half-clothed in corner shoved,
A ring inscribed by someone's once beloved.
These things were even here loved for a time,
Yet now such things have lost the old sublime.
As memory has faded in twilight,
The land of children lost like ammonites.
For here at evolution's zenith peak,
No death, no birth, no place left for the weak.

Pandæmonium
Third Circle

From the museum into garden downs,
The forms of life man brought here in the brown.
Small weeds and grasses to their arbours cling;
A few small flowers most could barely bring.
Chaotically their petal patterns spin,
No Fibonacci influence within.
A tape-recorded birdsong cycling
In amber lights, the life recycling
As filtered liquid up through muddy pipes,
In just enough for every genotype.
As ants make vicious war in stone and dirt,
Their tribalism locked in feudal hurt.
Survival of the fittest raging on:
A struggle man has never grown beyond.
So rare do I visit these vestiges,
For earth has no place in percentages.
And my appreciation in the green
Is cut by the stagnation so obscene.
For underpopulated, overgrown,
Frustrated, seasonless in winter groans.
No flourishing and no diminishing,
Immortal forms and no relinquishing.
This deathless city shall always endure,
As man is crowned and nature is cured.

Pandæmonium
Fourth Circle

Leaving the garden down volcanic stones,
I spiralled through alleys and little thrones.
Chaotic words, signals untraceable,
United babble untranslatable.
The tower of the cluttering city
Is stretching high, useless necessities;
Passing down of the temple souvenirs,
Still dropping down below the lamp veneer
Under the distant and unwaning moon,
That barely beams over the neon runes.
The pipes and cogs all choke the grease and smoke,
As rats and ravens in the puddles soak.
A coffin carver with a toothless grin,
Still working in this land where death is thin.
Today's new circulation hung like slate
Of words that we no longer propagate.
New stores adjoining to the old backbone,
A curtain red which muffles secret moans.
At last our love and sex have been divorced,
No embryonic obligation forced.
It's long since I dabbled in love and lust,
The physical as empty as the dust.
The heat of my heartbeat long sacrificed,
For there is no sharing in paradise.

Pandæmonium
Fifth Circle

I made my way through brothels blabbering,
And down laneways of bottles glimmering
To ruins of the public sector old,
An ancient place once grand now turned to mould.
A city built on good intentions here:
That dream of hope now but a souvenir.
I roamed through hospitals that rose like bones,
And welfare buildings crumbling like stones.
Small bastions of religion holding hope,
Which turned to ash as wiser men awoke.
For in unending night what use is light,
Redundant now the need of prophet sight.
Those first arrivals from the former place,
With grace they sought to serve their fellow race.
And yet so hard it was to work unpaid,
Eventually the population swayed.
For hospitals meant not much without death,
And welfare waved until there was none left.
The beggars here just an eternal curse,
They starve and take and never reimburse.
I used to think mercy was a virtue,
But where in sharing is the revenue?
For justice pays our way in this city,
For strength eternal and lost is pity.

Pandæmonium
Sixth Circle

Continuing down streets of compromise,
There roamed some vagabonds with rambling eyes,
Their eyes searching for ancient memories.
So few return in these late centuries.
The street dwellers began to coalesce,
And in their touch I felt myself regress.
I came here often in my early days,
When grief and hope had filled these alleyways;
Just after that great schism opened wide,
And theories of time and space denied.
So many lost to that great mystery,
Who never found their way to this city.
There rose a great tall monolith of slate,
A monument to those none could locate.
A database of those we once held dear,
Who never found their way to us in here.
The names ran up the base towards the clouds;
In muscle memory my head was bowed.
Unto the name so long ago I scribed,
And yet I felt as if my soul had died.
For standing here after so many years,
My wife in name to me would not appear;
Nor to my recollection came her grace,
Nor could my memory recall her face.

Pandæmonium
Seventh Circle

A little pang of guilt and touch of grief:
For which my apathy brought some relief.
For marriage, that dead institution lost.
Perfected evolution has a cost.
And yet so true I felt that sting of pain,
So I continued down the grimy drains.
And soon the water pulled me in her bite;
I longed against reason to end the night.
My purple suit now torn and faecal stained,
My hunger tiring into yearning strange.
My feelings bound me like an immigrant;
I yearned for home and pleasures ignorant.
But maybe in these pipes and aqueducts
I can find something which to reconstruct:
A new visage with which to see myself,
A stomach new to feast upon my wealth.
And yet none came in this labyrinth of filth,
Except a distant sound hard to distil.
Unquantifiable my length of route,
Below the water table so dilute.
And soon that distant sound became a cry,
Accusing me, and I no alibi.
And as the pitch became unbearable,
I found a commune deep and terrible.

Pandæmonium
Eighth Circle

I swam ashore from filth to filthy crowd,
Whose subjects desolate and naked bowed.
Some hospital gowns worn like ancient cloth,
Their veins pulsating with injected froth.
Some self-inflicting noble savages,
So drunk on the opiate of masses,
Flaming blaze their teeth with chatter and gnash,
Their words like broken pottery and ash.
"We tried" one cried "to build Utopia,
A city state; a cornucopia."
As several circled round a burning shrine,
Their groans were deep over the bread and wine.
These good people whose virtues turned to vice:
They know much more than I of paradise.
I saw within their hearts our happiness
Is seldom far apart from emptiness.
The cavern groaned in deepest agony;
Their elegy grotesque and out of key
Arose in song from city's darkest pits.
If only surface dwellers could hear it.
Their mourning true their life from lies unbound;
For this kingdom of rats is upside down.
Within these flames I found my piety,
Something sublime was closer to me.

Pandæmonium
Ninth Circle

Down through masses with newfound piousness,
As blood and violence filled the diocese,
I sought for that long fabled serpent throne,
Where that ancient worm must now burn alone.
I spiralled deeper down the burning pit
Past churches derelict and counterfeit,
Until I reached the deepest of domains,
In where I thought would be the darkest reign.
Yet there a kingless throne of peasant flight,
All clambering towards a tiny light.
For an oasis was that touch of sun,
That by the pagan slaughter overrun.
So beautiful that tiny window light,
That I was drawn up through the desperate fight.
And I for one moment the surface saw,
As clawed I was back to the furnace floor.
How hideous this kingdom to me now,
That by true light my eyes have been endowed.
And turning back I saw the path I laid:
I thought I had gone down in my crusade.
But here in contrast stood at highest peak,
With but one choice most hideous and bleak:
To live in sight of the sublime from hell,
Or go back down in ignorance to dwell.

The Death of Kama and Skanda

Distant bells signal the morning mantra,
Chanting the death of Kama and Skanda.
In our pious prayers of propaganda,
Reciting happiness memoranda.

In leaving each to their own odyssey,
Veneration of trivialities.
For in the safety of neutrality
Is the sweet colourless equality.

To mankind's self-sufficiency we swore;
In our timeless wisdom we banished war.
Holiday homes on the paradise shores,
And judgement banished to the ocean floor.

Yet inside the trees where we once were found,
Our momentary lives were inter-bound.
Connection was evolution's playground;
Relationship stood us up on the ground.

The Death of Kama and Skanda

All those thirty thousand years forgotten,
Inside the tail flick of a robin.
As sorrow and solitude begotten,
And housed in the modern grey and rotten.

Goddamn the bells! And everything they sell!
For this world they built is a living hell.
That love and indifference could indwell,
Is nothing but a siren's deadly spell.

For all true happiness lies between us,
Just as joy forms in our grief and distress.
For romance warms between Mars and Venus;
Lust is anything less or in excess.

The Babel Poet

Translated from Proto-Tamil
The truth to you in form I educate,
And never will I lie, equivocate.
My holy mantra subjectivity,
My true enchanter relativity.
To render translucent dissembling,
These metaphors from their resembling.
In languid empty thoughts proclivity,
My mind's quiescence in liquidity.
In meditation melancholy free,
Conceptualising evanescently.

Translated from Sanskrit
Far too quixotic for the odyssey,
Too embryonic for this sophistry;
For a cacophony of caustic verse
Is more prophet-able into my purse.
I speak where esoteric masses meet
In litanies of my molasses sweet.
For placid language is my sword and shield,
Her flaccid forms in strength and might I wield.
For absinth sublimates the saccharine,
Each absent thought abscission in decline.
In mellowness and meaningless I dwell,
No cosmic dissonance in distant bells.

The Babel Poet

Translated from Sumerian
Like coelacanth in evolution's sea,
Unchanged in the abyssal reverie.
The void verbose and the obscenities,
Within my poetry a rarity.
No dabbling in neologism,
For poetry is parallelism.
Ephemeral are my epiphanies,
In paradoxes and toxicities.
My eyes are closed when effulgence is bright,
For I am symbiosis with moonlight.

Translated from Neo-Babylonian
As splinters and elixirs oscillate,
As form and shape like cinder abdicate.
For life is but reflection of the mind,
And the subscription to a mind like mine.
My substance of resistance, foam and sand,
My coexistence in subsistence stands.
To men my words are the Rosetta Stone,
In disbelief I cast the crackled bones.
A little ink so dark and crystalline,
A little wormwood makes my paper shine.
Within my tower gold and ivory,
Where I seance to like society.

Tenochtitlan
Part 1: Montezuma II

The tears of the sun were stolen,
    as the earth with blood became swollen.
Bloodied slaves led to barbarous lands
    through serpentine sands.
Desert ruins, cruel and cold,
    pave the path to beauty untold.
A desert blue oasis,
    crowned by a red city rapacious.
Ancient hate finds eminence
    in temples of cosmic elegance.

Slaves pushed through the opulence,
    bathed in bloody sacraments.
Woman clothed in jade
    men wield obsidian blades.
Hypnotic noise and crowd,
    blue paint endowed.
Writhing in the ecstasy
    of sacrificial miquiztli.
Civilised savagery
    palpitates in fervent piety.

Tenochtitlan
Part 1: Montezuma II

Covenant intensity
    at the stairs of ascendancy;
Driven up the blood-stained stones,
    to chanting throne.
Silence cries out
    as demon dancers wait devout.
The blue-bodied shiver,
    The feathered prophet quivers.
Sacrifice is drawn:
    knife is raised like darkest dawn.

Cries erupt as knife starts slitting;
    Screams as ribs start splitting.
Heart held throbbing to the skies,
    the Blood Debt paid in cries.
Seated above and satiated,
    Moctezuma by gods ingratiated.
Quetzalcoatl again shall rise;
    By blood the city evades demise.
Tenochtitlan bound in dark fellowship
    under the fear of apocalypse.

Tenochtitlan
Part II: Cortés

Over purgatory's seas
  from the curve of eternity
To a jungle shore
  where milk and honey pour.
Genesis opened again,
  her wealth to be the claim of Spain.
Our virginal sacrifice
  in the conquest of paradise.
Seizing savage pleasures,
  ravaged beyond measure.

Cutting up, through Satan's stronghold,
  to a city of gold untold.
A water world in grandeur
  beyond imaginable splendour.
Rising monolithic stones
  outshining even Castile's thrones.
Crowned in pagan godhood,
  paraded through the city northward.
Brought to the temple walls,
  where amazement became fear and gall.

Tenochtitlan
Part II: Cortés

The stench of fresh sacrifice
        putrefying Eden's paradise.
For this unholy sight one choice remains:
        divine damnation shall reign.
In our swords is salvation,
        and we the angels of civilisation.
Infidels torn apart:
        steel through their savage hearts.
Curing their savagery
        with black religious barbarity.

Genocidal blood spilt,
        penance to counteract the guilt.
The rape of the citadel
        buried all the children who dwelled.
The feathered serpent crushed underfoot;
        city oasis turned to soot.
The apocalyptic violence
        Turns to sorrowful silence.
And in the fight for forbidden fruit
        Eden is once again left destitute.

Poltergeists
Introduction

Grief will not forever sleep;
Cocooned the chrysalid will not keep.
Once again Chernobyl speaks
Through butterflies and Geiger beeps.
Amber rises from the deep
As creatures once extinct now leap.
Poets rhyme and mothers weep
On the day memory shall reap.
Some in kindness some in shrieks,
As Poltergeists descend the peaks.

Poltergeists
Amber

Two serpentine eyes flittering, at the Cretaceous sun, dizzying.
Her first sight, since her hatching night, little scales glistening the light.
Dwarfed by her mother's peeled skin as she leaves her clutch of sibling kin.
Legless running through the branches by little raptors feathered dances.
A little Eve of serpent tree, who sadly selected not to be.
As sap, in evil opulence, formed her dark amber sarcophagus.
In liquid gold was agonised and her drowning form was crystallised.
Beautified, as by death was filled, and deposited gently, like silt,
As glided her family tree through extinction to eternity.
Yet still her half-life lingers on, refused her place in the great bygone.
Castaway in a timeless rift, sailing on the continental drift.
Until one day rediscovered, by primate hands, was cut and numbered.
To men she was a gallery; her glass cage, naked opacity:
Her suspended animation without a waking inhalation.
Yet before her endless exile, she was a queen among reptiles;
Now just a curiosity in the mammalian odyssey.
Displayed like a stain glass window, this little poltergeist in limbo.

Poltergeists
Ultrasound

Dawn
A gentle breeze through an open window,
Golden dust caught in the sunlight below.
Empty
The sun raises no warmth within this room,
For in gold amber we have been entombed:
An altar raised atop the windowsill,
An ultrasound that's now forever still.
Sorrow
In all the things that did not come to be,
Turning this house into an ossuary.
Dusk.

Death
Grief turning family to progeny,
Travelling deep though the shared memory.
Forming
Grief once tasted lingers on like absinthe,
Like a lost child roaming a labyrinth,
Her little voice which never grows older,
Whispering softly over my shoulder.
Slowly
The butterfly that I had been denied,
In her chrysalid form she'll never die.
Life.

Poltergeists
Ultrasound

Cold
When I first met you between the sunrays,
Where I for tears could not see past the fray.
Horror
When unconsidered grief takes form and voice,
And yet soon her voice came to fill the void;
And so I gently filled the home anew,
Hallways and windows with new life imbued.
Changing
As I made up a little room for her,
Making my little poltergeist daughter
Warm.

Poltergeists
Chernobyl Lynx

A spotted lynx moves slow through silver snow,
Her huntress eyes so wide and wondrous.
Her shifting fur is crowned by her surrounds,
By streams, which flow on tides of cyanide.
Yet her instincts, free of long memory,
Oblivious to the oblivion.
The name of Chernobyl to her remains,
Something only other creatures whisper.
The metropolis and sarcophagus,
Her nursery home, and all that is known.
For she is but a child of the wild;
No place in memory for tragedy,
Be it in innocence or ignorance,
Moves joyfully, through lands of atrophy.
Her poltergeist form, turning winter warm.

Poltergeists
Poetry

Poetry
Changing in imagination.
Delving deep the depths of the mind,
Constructing the now from what's behind.
The strange half-life in which we dwell,
Rebuilding Chernobyl's Citadel.
Raising Atlantis from the sea; and replanting El Dorado's trees.
As the past now fills the present, and the laws of time and space are bent.
Yet with each passing metaphor, the Geiger beeps just a little more.
For I am not a citizen,
And hauntingly don't belong therein.
Chernobyl, now a paradise,
Shall never be shed of sacrifice
And man's unchanging frailty.
Poetry.

Poltergeists
Poetry

Alchemy
Turns day to night in memory.
With every touch some turns to gold,
And a little more to spoil's hold.
For there is no preservation,
Inevitable desecration.
For what is joy in the morrow, by this midnight may well be sorrow.
Spinning the amber time machine; spinning winter back to summer green.
Leaves fall up to skeleton trees, and autumn becomes a travesty.
Where once there was some certainty,
Memory becomes illusory.
As Midas tries to civilise,
In the end can but cannibalise.
In the rewritten history:
Alchemy.

Poltergeists
Poetry

Poltergeists
Overturn stones in paradise.
Ghosts in a world material,
Physical invades the spiritual.
A small moment of boyhood joy,
I cut and prune like it's a toy.
Picking through the ancient ashes, shifting sand upon tidal splashes.
Past tragedies newly imbued, with the present's false solicitude.
In rearranging ancient rooms, clumsily opening amber tombs.
Even myself in memory:
I have long outgrown like willow trees.
And the world that I remember
My words beautify and dismember.
Some I bless, some I sacrifice.
Poltergeists.

Día de los Muertos Part I: Day of the Dead

1

The dawn she breaks upon the land of breath
      Where nation's grief transforms to jubilee,
      And sorrow raptures into ecstasy.

This land alive in vibrant pulsing life
      As colors circle into energy,
      And beauty forms of the grotesquery.

The living dance in joy with spectral dead
      In graveyards marigolds lay musically,
      As the community sings elegies.

2

The people of the sun in blinding light
      As human grief flows universally
      And blooms in Catholic Aztec unity.

Tequila, toys and songs on altars raised
      For life is lived in death's affinity;
      Dividing line is but illusory.

The dead had lived aware of the divine
      Inside Quetzalcoatl's sanctity
      And bound to Mary in her pageantry.

3

For under calacas the people blind
      For under feasting lies the fallacy
      Of turning death into a fantasy.

The dead are not so easily appeased
      For mortals we cannot so easily
      Abstract from death and grief their gravity.

For death will not be bound to but one day
      Nor mar the lines of faith so carelessly.
      These streets are crowded empty piety.

Día de los Muertos Part II: Night of the Living

1
The night she falls so cold on those with breath
      As marble black and white fall heavily,
      As sorrow circles the grey hauntingly.

Inside this land of solitary life
      Emotions veiled by the pleasantry,
      Placebo curtains hide intensity.

The living hide in fear of spectral dead
      As vain the sermon words fall gracelessly,
      As if the lost had lived so faithfully.

2
The living lost in moon's so murky light
      The proud agnostic dead unwillingly
      Is baptized in religiosity.

The elegy so maudlin is she raised
      As bitter grief in swallowed eulogy:
      A life reduced to trivialities.

The dead in life had none of the divine
      To ignorance we move eternity;
      Judge not the dead in their mortality.

3
For under their denial people blind
      A meagre table food and remedy,
      As living wake the dead to destiny,

Our grief is not so easily appeased
      As enemies make light with family,
      Our funerals enforce the harmony.

Forbidding death her voice in light of day
      Eternal grief expels the progeny
      To walk through grief alone in misery.

Truth Set Sail
Part I

Obelisks and pyramids
All line the streets and city grids,
Casting sandstone shadows dark
Over the shallows cold and stark.
Heavenly their nighttime glow
Upon the lake reflecting low.

Gazed from sleepy sunlit shores,
These ziggurats that have no doors.
Facing brothels all in bloom,
As shamans grovel in the gloom.
Ancient tombs in carven runes,
Like some forgotten desert dunes.

Standing here majestic vast,
Yet all their former glory passed.
Cathedrals alone in stone,
From where salvation never roams,
Carved into the citadels,
Yet with the people do not dwell.

Monastery mountain peaks.,
A solitary faith won't speak.
Monuments that meet the sky,
Yet hunched beside the homeless lie.
Surely was the widow's mite
That paid for this majestic sight.

Truth Set Sail
Part I

Blacking the shining sun
A shine to sign what man has done.
Marble columns to the sky
Are marvelled by the passerby.
Yet these riches render poor,
When souls are sold for nothing more.

Stone ornate against the sky,
Complexity did daze my eyes.
Caught in the reflected light
Of colours shining from on height.
Truly here is majesty:
The stained window nativity.

In agate and quartz there shone
The king foretold and promised one.
And below a doorway dark,
That drew in daylight cold and stark,
With it all and naught to lose,
I went in looking for the truth.

Truth Set Sail
Part II

Welcomed through the cold slipway,
By druids on commission pay.
With a jewel-encrusted cross
And golden rings countless in cost.
Robes all lined with charms and spells,
His hide a haunch where demons dwell.

Eyes so lifeless blind to me,
A sea of souls he doesn't see.
Once there lived here fishermen,
And yet to merchants now a den.
Once a boat and olive grove,
More than enough for truth to flow.

Now all wealth and opulence
Robs truth from the acropolis.
Standing countless in the crowd,
Which spirals daily reendowed.
Marble pillars carrying
The distant ceiling dizzying.

Wonder at the work of man
At every rock hewn by our hands
To the worlds of art above
Of olive branches, mercy doves.
Beautiful the brush and stroke,
And yet by them no soul awoke.

Truth Set Sail
Part II

None sought meaning in the sky,
For we in deadly slumber lie.
Sleep this sleep so hard to shake,
Harder than iron is to break.
Further in through crowd was drawn,
Unto an altar weathered worn.

Inlaid in the ivory,
The hieroglyphs tell history
That the future has forgot,
As all the scriptures left to rot.
And I bowed and read the word,
Misunderstood yet ever heard.

Bring your sins and sacraments,
And weep to sleep your soul's lament.
So I gave my tourist coin,
As queuing for the exit joined
Leaving with salvation stowed
And yet the truth was not bestowed.

Truth Set Sail
Part III

In the library Babel text,
I sought for truth in babble sect.
Majesty and alchemy
Were woven in the tapestry.
Lectures long and grandiose,
The architecture filled with boast.

"Sleep now subjective is truth,
In our perspective past reproof.
Truth in death is then defied,
For with their writer words will die.
Sleep for no immortal stands,
And truth is banished from this land."

Lost in endless chattering,
And wisdom's words so dazzling.
Yet of truth I could find none,
And in that thought the sleep undone.
And the mystery of night,
Was rotten by the morning light.

The verbose and comatose
Upon themselves all overdose.
Wisdom sought for nowhere else,
Like serpents feeding on themselves.
From their pulpit song of lies,
The vipers sing their lullabies.

Truth Set Sail
Part III

Cynicism of the wise,
As mysticism mystifies.
What would you say in the day
That an immortal is displayed?
Truth, yes truth, she does not sleep,
But through eternity will keep.

And the great incarnate voice
Will not always extend you choice.
How long will the truth be bled
By all these voices of the dead?
Truth, O Truth, why do you stay,
In these foundations weak as clay?

Hopelessness O! Hopelessness,
This land of vain self-righteousness.
Will the truth forever weep
For those who will not wake from sleep?
How long will the truth be grieved
Before the light decides to leave?

Truth Set Sail
Part IV

Yet a voice called from the east,
A wilderness that yearned release.
Ancient lands now freedom-less,
A kingdom that is seasonless.
So the truth took mast and sail
Like a majestic caravel.

To the east over the seas,
Into a land of desert trees,
Truth set foot among the thorns,
Where garden lands to desert worn
Was a land so desolate
The ground so dry and summer baked.

Rivers naught but empty streams,
Of spring was none but winter's dream.
Ancient paths once laid in stone,
Where wolves and jackals make their home.
Yet into the streams and springs
The truth began her whispering.

Over hills of rocky soil,
The clouds now cooled what Sun did boil.
And the sky once blistering,
The chimes of rain were now singing.
And over the desert land,
The truth laid out his blooming hand.

Truth Set Sail
Part IV

And the trees of ancient years
Did bloom again as truth drew near.
And from branches dry as bone
The desert roses made a throne.
Flowering the fig and trees,
So heavy now fruit laden leaves.

As the baobab seeds awoke,
New seedlings sprung as winter broke,
As the ibex and the fox
Came from the highlands in their flocks.
And descending with the rain,
There came the hawk, egret and crane.

Beautifully their voices sing,
Just like the holy seraphim.
And upon their melodies,
The truth sang out so merrily.
And from thorns a vineyard grew,
Whose wine did taste of holy truth.

Nurtured by sweet Nature

Seasonal Meditations
Winter

Four Monarchs
Upon the once leaf-laden ground,
In grief our maiden royal found.
She waltzes in through weather cold,
In jolts she takes her reign to hold.
Her population all subdued,
A cease to creation ensued.
Her crown of icy glass anew
Was gowned again in coldest coup.
Her predecessor sadly killed,
From splendour red to blue was filled.
And yet within their formal seals:
A kinship clouds could not conceal.
For queens did weave in threads' descent,
As green soon leaves in cold lament.
The aching kingdom silent still,
Awaiting ransom to be filled:
A queen arising yellow tides,
With wattle green her joyous stride.

Seasonal Meditations
Winter

Winter Work
The road by night in winter storm,
As autumn moon is shifting form.
In vengeful clouds of dark intent,
Now fill the town with cold lament.
So slow to rise is morning light;
No birds to sing away the night.
The ceaseless cycle, sleep and work,
So little sun to lift the murk.
As shadows fill the shallows deep,
My mind but barely lifts from sleep.
The chorus of my working day,
My porous heart so little sway.
As countless words move in my soul,
And yet each day I am less whole.

Seasonal Meditations
Spring

"As the days begin to shorten with the arrival of autumn the Monarchs begin to fly south. As they go their numbers increase until they form great processions. In spring they set off northwards. The majority stopped to breed in the south and then died, leaving their offspring to continue their journey to the north where their parents had hatched as caterpillars. It's one of the most impressive sights in the whole of nature."
David Attenborough

1
Winter long had filled my mind,
Her distant verses cold, unkind.
Embers which I gave no care,
All vanishing like mist in air.
Winter jaws which barely rhyme,
A scattering of thoughts in time.
Reminiscing of the past…

~

*My infancy entirely
Wrapped in the immediacy
Of touch and taste and sight and sound.
All sweetness laced and light abounds,
Where choice and instinct are the same,
Where Grief and Guilt are left unnamed.
No past and no futurity
In days before my memory.
Yet seasons born so quickly die,
Just as the monarch butterflies.*

~

Seasonal Meditations
Spring

2

Similes of long-lost spring,
Nostalgia in her costly sting.
Happiness so rarely lives
In the reflections winter gives
In her cold reality
Of whispering mortality.
Grieving deep in sadder words…

~

Summer lost in shivering,
In teeth of winter withering.
Mission now complete for me,
Save my omission over sea.
Grieve me not as lost but found,
For with my Lord I am now bound
Spring eternal eagle wings!
A youthful song to heaven bring!

~

Seasonal Meditations
Spring

3

Words they flow from joy to grief,
Despondent souls yearn for relief,
Longing for that brighter morn
In poetry as clear as dawn.
And maybe un-mystery,
These fragmentary words in me.
Struggling to understand…

~

The summer sun so spins upon the shores
Of turquoise tides all tossing in their tune,
As sandstone smoothed by swell all spiralling,
That pillars purple in parabolas.
As ceaselessly she calls companionship,
For modern man in his meandering,
Ellipsis in emerging of eclipse,
No home and halo have humanity.

~

Seasonal Meditations
Spring

4

Soon upon the wind a change:
The monarch butterflies in range.
Mind from slumber now awake,
My chrysalid cocoon did break.
Focus growing sharper in,
As winter rolls and spring begins.
Little stanzas taking shape…

~

These moments spiral in parabolas.
Two desperate forms together find shape,
As newlyweds keep warm as moonlight breaks,
Path to love a garden of memory.

~

5

Uncocooned at last from night,
A million monarchs in the light.
Spring, so delicate her eyes,
As countless creatures rhapsodize.
I within her warm embrace:
At last I find a moment's grace.
Thoughts now take their final forms,
As Saturn's lead to gold reforms.
Butterflies on forest floor,
Their wings became my metaphor.
Spring ascends from winter skies
As scattered thoughts together rise.
Thus arose leviathan…

Seasonal Meditations
Summer

Seasons
Four worlds spin and dance. Men by them entranced,
Stored in each the forms of calmness and storms.
Those few who open to winter frozen,
Composed in the leaves and skeleton trees.
Others favour change in autumn arranged,
Lovers there are some who love most spring sun.
Yet I
Driven by passion to summer fashion,
Given to the heat where sea and sun meet.
All the earth to me opportunity,
Called through the daylight, as late draws the night.
Filled by desire, December fire,
Distilling heaven, Summer ascension.
And yet
Heat of summer days in endless array
Cheats the cooling hand of autumn's command.
For summer adorned like a rose in thorns,
More heat than the earth can turn to rebirth.
Embers burst to flame. Growth by ash is stained,
Rendering all progress into regress.
Therefore
All the four quartets, coupling duets,
Call the year to tune in drought and monsoon.
Just as fades folly to melancholy,
Thrusts autumns colour: lyrical slumber.
Dark hymns of winter scatter and splinter,
Stark contrast her verse as Spring is dispersed.
Summer.

Seasonal Meditations
Autumn

Summer.
Sun of innocence, her world so immense.
Summer, blessed Summer.
Ceaseless energy cycling the sea,
Painting the picture of life's elixir.
Summer, ascending Summer.
Fills me up porous, my form amorphous.
Nothing fixed in me, countless things to be.
Pure innocence, no experience,
Summer, fading Summer.
The long-dreaded end, claiming my old friend.
That trepidation, Autumn's formation,
Summer.
To thy sweet presence, Death seemed thy absence.

Seasonal Meditations
Autumn

Autumn.
From summer so warm, I had feared your form,
Autumn, dreaded Autumn.
Summer now begets, memory regrets,
Choice diminishes, as day finishes,
Autumn, desolate Autumn.
The Sun's effulgence, passions less intense
A little older, life growing colder.
Summer's clarity, now illusory.
Autumn, changing Autumn.
In long gone solstice, a strange warm solace.
In thy consequence, lies true cognizance,
Autumn.
Now within thy hold, new wisdom enfolds.

Seasonal Meditations
Autumn

Autumn.
Age melancholic, youth embryonic.
Autumn, newfound Autumn.
Cursed once seemed to me, thy skeleton trees;
Yet beneath the leaves, thy beauty cleaves,
Autumn, beautiful Autumn.
For thy Summer sun, Autumn moon are one;
From sweet innocence to experience:
Two not disparate, but of one spirit,
Autumn, joyful Autumn.
Summer held alone a childish throne,
Autumn by itself robbed of inner wealth,
Autumn.
Heart of innocence forms experience.

Wright Valley Seals

Some three thousand years in a land as this,
Twists hopes and fears of history to mist.
Here each grain of sand, without wind to lift,
Moves less than the land's continental drift.
Such is the stillness of this solitude
Without a witness to decrepitude.

Lost particles course the unfaithful sky;
The sun long divorced from the cold and dry.
As light and dark dance without syzygy,
A desert entranced with infinity.
The blush of dawn is gifted to others,
As darkness is drawn and love is smothered.

The very landscape is contemplation;
Her thoughts take shape in stern desolation.
Like some formless mind, unknowable dark,
Through the cold she climbed in cruelty so stark.
Dark corpses and stone grotesquely adorn,
Bowing to her throne in night without dawn.

Wright Valley Seals

Nothing breathes or bleeds, no inhabitant.
Life itself recedes into banishment.
Even death is strange in this shapeless place,
Memories arranged, embalmed without grace.
Corpses of seals like flies in amber,
Too cold to feel the death they clamber.

Through the centuries came the lost creatures,
Cast from seven seas and icy beaches.
Their bodies tribute to the gallery,
Their bones distribute dark duality.
Twilight eternal, their forms unageing:
To death infernal forever raging.

For death is sacred inside this dark place,
The seals who bled across time and space.
Preserved and displayed like kings of mortals,
Their last breath is stayed ever immortal.
As maggots consume the corpses of men,
The grief of this tomb forever extends.

Water-Dragon

Down through the dark and desolate cement,
Past triple lanes of traffic and torment,
Chalkstone covered by cape ivy crisscross,
A pathway painted by pebble and moss.

    Sheltered from sun in a cave of sandstone,
    Hewn and hollowed in hues of honeycomb,
    Wakes a wild baby water-dragon,
    Eyes beaming and bolting through the bracken.

        Ravenous hunger, red rapacious,
        A creature cast out of the Cretaceous,
        In shady sun he shimmers and flickers,
        In the masonic marble he mirrors.

            Gondwana's gift of green-eyed oddities,
            Tributaries of the Triassic tree,
            Lingering here in the limestone and leaves,
            As the sunlight in his scales is seized.

Pan

Underneath the weight of industry,
And far beneath the slate antiquity.
Fossilised by the disdain of man,
There lie the petrified remains of Pan.
With his eyes of stone and pipe of dust,
His song lies in bones and love lies in lust.
The span of his majestic beauty
Man long rejected for utility.
Gaia calls out romantic impulse,
A pariah in our frantic repulse.
Progress in the price of gasoline:
Nature's regress a sacrifice foreseen,
As all ancient wisdom is silenced,
Made vacant for the kingdom of science.
Left with just one verdict so tragic,
We are the death of Pan's perfect magic.

Es Vedrà Part I: Creation (The Forming of The Island)

Born before the birth of time,
There climbed in crags a coastal line.
Inlets in her isles meet,
Where flowers flourish, fair and sweet.
Sea was wrapped in sunlit spray,
As buds did bloom beside the bay.
Reefs in blush beyond the brink
Of coloured coral now extinct.
Through which countless creatures crawled,
An ancient sunken city sprawled.

Hunters hover from on high,
Their wings of silver shimmer sky.
The continual collide
Of seas in timeless turning tides,
Waging war with waves and waves
That carved the cornered cliffs and caves.
Monuments and monoliths,
Before mankind had moved through myth.
Still the sea dissatisfied,
She sought herself the high hillside.

So to satiate the sea,
The earth erupted violently.
Through the rock a rumbling,
In toppling and tumbling.
And through countless centuries,
The fragments from foundation freed,
Creation continuing
In perfect pruning perfuming.
Crumbled cliffs all casting down,
To beds of reef becoming bound.

Es Vedrà Part I: Creation (The Forming of The Island)

Slipping into sea the stone,
The tides in turn now take their throne.
Forces carved and cut the coast
Unto the islands innermost.
Still there stood a single shape
Of bedrock bold that would not break.
For her stone so held the sky,
So that they held their hillsides high.
Column up in colour crowned,
In birds and beauty she was bound.

Carven as a cathedral,
Perfected in the primeval,
Still the sea was satisfied,
Despite the rock that was denied.
Though the steeple had been saved,
Was there she worshipped with her waves
Singing soft and shimmering
On rocks that round the island ring.
By eternity was touched,
Before the man was drawn from dust.

Es Vedrà Part II: Temptation (Sirens and Odysseus)

Sailing through the siren sea,
Protected by a prophecy,
Sailors saved by wax stood fast,
As rope restrained me round the mast.
Soft across the sea did sing,
In rolling rhythm start to ring.
Rock arose from water's rush
Where blooming beauty lay and blushed.
And the words once whispering,
Like gold was glowing, glittering.

Then I saw upon the shore,
In splendour like the starlit stores,
Figures like two flowers dressed,
That were in beauty bound and blessed.
Vivid voices vexing me,
As starlight shivers on the sea;
Breath which blew in from their breasts,
So sung my soul to sacred rest.
Eyes elusive entering,
My soul from spring to wintering.

Longing for their lips of lies,
For they of heaven's honour cry,
To bestow me bold and brave,
The spoils sweet for which I slaved.
Music wrapped in dark mystique,
A slithering of serpent speak.
Yet my honour is at home,
When I return from rugged roam.
From their lies I looked away,
For their seduction held no sway.

Es Vedrà Part II: Temptation (Sirens and Odysseus)

Yet their tongues now turned to Troy,
With such temptation now they toyed,
Whispering of wretched war,
And Ithaca's most inner shore.
Precious most Penelope,
For ten years truly thought of thee;
Slowly slipping to their spell,
In hunger for my home to dwell.
Yet then dawned on me demise,
For lust I knew is laid in lies.

The veneer of visage bled,
And I in horror hung my head.
All their filthy flesh was flayed,
The depths of dismay and decay;
Stench which slithered through the sea,
Their mouths which moaned in misery.
Bodies once in beauty bound,
Now in disease and death were drowned.
Through the sea we splashed and sailed,
As withered witches left to wail.

Es Vedrà Part III: Fall (Sacrifices to Tanit)

Darkness draws as daylight drains,
The shore and stones in sorrow stained.
Sundown signs a sacrifice
Upon the shore the sacred site.
Full moon flashes on the flesh
Of countless cut and beating chest.
Demons dance in dissonance,
So vile their veins and virulent.
Frantic frenzied fervour night
That marks a mother murder rite.

Clutching close the chosen child,
A worshipper so warped and wild.
Time has come for tortured tears,
Ferocious flames in flowing fear.
Pain eternal ecstasy,
And death divine in devilry.
Darkened heads all dance and dip,
As sacrifice is struck and stripped:
Blind in faith fertility,
As blood is drawn barbarity.

Anguish and all agony,
The mother moans in misery.
Soul in sorrow deeply steeped,
As life to sea is slowly seeped.
Little life is lynched away,
The savages by slaughter sway.
Tanit god and tyrant king,
Veracious veneration bring.
Bathe the dawn in baby blood,
And favour us with fertile flood.

Es Vedrà Part III: Fall (Sacrifices to Tanit)

Flames and fire fade away,
And silence takes all sound to slay.
Dawn descends on darkest death;
Just smoking sand and soot is left.
Sunlight shares no solace here,
In cold and cruel we cry austere.
The horrific humbled down,
As rush reduced to rabble sound
To a soul to schism lost
In cataclysmic conscience cost,

Greed of god for grief and guilt,
So racks regret and robs relief.
Sons upon the slaughter stones,
Our daughters dark in death dethroned.
Where our weary women weep,
Our men by misery made meek.
This is Tanit's testament,
His endless empty banishment
As cascading currents cry,
As blood from rolling rapids rise.

Es Vedrà Part IV: Redemption (Francisco Palau)

Travelling in thought through time,
From castaway sweet chapel mine.
Boyhood born in battlegrounds,
My country was in conflict crowned.
Yet from youth I gave to you,
My trust and faith for you are true.
Going where His glory calls,
To follow where faith doesn't fall.
Firm in faith and fortitude,
Yet always seeking solitude.

Thus my life was torn in two,
Between the world and when withdrew.
This exile it eats away
These desolate and drifting days.
Body bent and bowed in age
In chains was cast to coastal cage.
Homesick in my heart and hands,
I long for Spain her song and sand.
Weathered hands worn by the war,
That time and tribulation tore.

Now my days by dunes will drain,
As perishing paroles my pain.
Sailing to a sandy beach,
I row to where the world can't reach:
Etching out exile in prayer,
Beyond the brink of land so bare.
I may find some piety,
In silence from society.
Seeking such sweet solitude,
As nurtured by sweet nature nude.

Es Vedrà Part IV: Redemption (Francisco Palau)

Up the shore of stone and sand,
To sanctum where my solace stands.
Sculpted cave of shade and sun,
Which draws me in when days are done.
Rain through rocky roof does fall,
And chimes this church like bells in call.
Bells I answer all alone
Inside this solitary stone.
Softly then the Spirit spoke,
To word and wisdom I awoke.

Long for solitude I searched,
Yet Christ in man he makes his church.
Bound and born in beauty blessed,
Yet stone delight not duty dressed.
This old steeple spiralled stone,
Is but a bed of barren bones.
Though my faith a fortitude,
Cannot survive in solitude.
For inside the make of man,
Does God pursue his perfect plan.

Word becomes Flesh

Coelacanth
Part I: To Wrestle with Stone

A musical romance of stone evolves,
As bone erotically shows her resolve.
A Coelacanth with ancient mortal wounds,
And petrified in underwater dunes.
In desecration Coelacanth was laid,
Soft preservation kept him undecayed.
The fossil image shimmers like a dance,
As Chaos waltzing Eros in a trance.
All nature's laws in fossil poetry,
Evoked from waters of a parted sea.
Palaeontologists with lovers' hands,
And prophet's eyes so gently etching sand.
As wrestling grit rejoins a broken hip,
Each cut so deepens the relationship.
In time their love and meditation meet;
Engagement becomes consummation sweet.
The stone and slate become the bone and scale,
As faint movement is seen within the tail.
A breath renewed now hovers in the deep,
The exodus of life in remnants keep.
At last the chaos of the visage storms,
Into the stone tablets' perfected form.

Coelacanth
Part II: Stone Made Flesh

Some fishermen dry wrestle fruitless night,
Their nets hung empty by the morning light.
Yet then there raptured the eternal depth,
A Coelacanth extinct yet full of breath.
A paradox within a parable,
This animal a living miracle.
His vice-less swim from prehistoric sea,
In purple skin of deepest family.
And yet the sailors' eyes, all veiled by scales,
In doubts they all deny beneath the sails.
Yet had they read the stone account could see,
Beneath humility lay majesty,
Unchanged from every fossil prophecy,
As evolution changing all the sea.
Up from the deep foundations of the earth,
This creature rose in resurrected worth.
The history of man and earth made clear,
The words of Coelacanth for those with ears.
As bioluminescence lit the night,
As fishermen in faith received their sight.
From wonderment to knowledge now confess,
The true magnificence of stone made flesh.

Reflections on the Apostles' Creed
The Paradox King

Born of the Virgin Mary

From starkest line of wretched kings,
Messiah somehow their offspring,
That their sin turns to perfect grace,
Prince of Peace in a war-torn race,
Prophets of word for God waiting,
Word becomes flesh our Paradox King.

Virgin birth of modest estate,
He who earth and stars did create
Contained within a child's eyes.
Infinity this baby's cry,
Divine descent of virgin womb,
Gifting man ascent from empty tomb.

Humility his human form,
Authority which stills the storm;
Complete is his duality,
In man's meekness and God's glory;
Both in fullness in Christ indwell,
That man may goodness again excel.

Reflections on the Apostles' Creed
The Paradox King

Disdainful day, accursed wood,
Shameful man slays immortal good.
Eternal One cries *It is done!*
As night empties the burning Son.
Crown of mockery men appraised,
Now crowned in Glory the King is raised.

Bled his blood for sinners to sing,
Our sinless praise to Servant King.
Grace unfurled our saviour brings,
Without end our Vanguardist King
To paradise, death without sting,
Eternal life, our Paradox King.

Reflections on the Apostles' Creed
Peter's Ascension

He ascended into heaven

I saw not the nails;
Nor spear impaled.
But saw my Lord's eyes;
With tears I denied.
That cross of hideous desolation,
Where friendship was drowned in dark temptation.
My shameful descent
Of my pride's intent
That without ascent,
Eternal torment,
No risen ascent
From deepest lament.

Yet upon the shore,
Like so long before,
A voice called to me
That once calmed this sea.
Never in me did guilt and joy so meet,
Then bowed, here and now, at my Saviour's feet.
Thrice the question came;
Forgiveness from shame.
Grace and ascension;
From sins descension.
Love and ascension
In Christ's accession.

Reflections on the Apostles' Creed
Peter's Ascension

To ends of the earth
Goes the rock-laid church,
As Christ from heaven
Forms new creation.
And I, bound where I do not want to go,
The cross, I once denied, by faith would know.
And as my life ends,
I will see my friend.
Death becomes to me
My ascendancy.
Jesus guiding me
In ascendency.

And until that day
Christ shall line our way
In tongues of fire
From heaven's spires.
For my friend sits upon the judgement seat;
So nought, but his will, shall his servants meet.
As countless are raised,
By his blood are saved.
For his ascension
Is our redemption.
In his ascension
Reigns our salvation.

Reflections on the Apostles' Creed
The Remnant Moon

The holy universal church

As I wondered by the bright midnight sea,
The tune of the remnant moon beamed on me.
And strange and sorrowful began her song,
For to fallen nature she once belonged.
A heart of stone enthroned in distant cold,
No beauty in her craters could I behold.

Yet the Sun, oh glorious majesty!
Arose that from shadows she might be free.
In dawning form he engaged her in light,
Banishing from her the face of the night.
And their love entwined beamed upon the earth,
And she, bound to Him, found reflected worth.

Over Jerusalem in full moon grace,
The tune of the Sun by the psalms were traced.
And even as her faith did wax and wane
In the night of Babylonian chains,
That faithful remnant, the sweet crescent moon,
In the blazing flame remembered the tune.

Reflections on the Apostles' Creed
The Remnant Moon

And again she became full and white,
Wedded to the risen Son, gowned in light.
Even the wings of the stars of heaven
Illuminated by her succession.
And her meekness and reflected beauty
Inherits the earth in Sun-bound duty.

And in the eternal dawn of the Sun,
That faithful remnant ascending as one.
The moon purified by the Sun's romance,
Eternity lit by their wedding dance.
And then the earth in both her hemispheres,
Was lit from heaven by the wedded spheres.

And I, clothed in darkness, dove in the wave,
And in reflected sunlight I was saved.
Baptised within the warmth of the moon's glow,
Rising above the water, white as snow.
By grace a citizen of remnant moon,
Ascending to sing the Sun's saving tune.

Poetry
Part I: Leviathan

"Canst thou draw out leviathan with an hook? or his tongue with a cord which thou lettest down? Canst thou put an hook into his nose? or bore his jaw through with a thorn? Will he make many supplications unto thee? will he speak soft words unto thee? Will he make a covenant with thee? wilt thou take him for a servant for ever? None is so fierce that dare stir him up: who then is able to stand before me?"

Job 41

There in the beginning was dark and void,
As silence rings the depths without a voice.
The ocean cauldron where all chaos stirred,
When Pneuma took up motion with the Word.
As one in form, poetic luminance,
The epic stormed throughout the universe.
And scattered stars which pulsate in their blaze,
Whose light from afar the Magi stargaze.
The navel of the Earth our paradise,
Yet to the deep our form has little worth.
And there within the deep the Spirit speaks,
And calls mystique among the ocean peaks.
A name which supplication does demands,
That subjugates and reigns the rock and sand.
His shadows cause the men to fear and pray,
In stalking shallows of the sailors lai.
Whose summoning enforces chaos quelled,
In the foundations of the Earth he dwells.
A realm which flashes tooth and jaw and tongue,
As his majestic fame by word was sung.
A twisted serpent, dragon of the sea,
Converging chaos passion majesty.
Both beauty violence in his soul to keep,
Leviathan his name and kingship deep.

Poetry
Part II: Behemoth

Behold now behemoth, which I made with thee; he eateth grass as an ox. Lo now, his strength is in his loins, and his force is in the navel of his belly. He moveth his tail like a cedar: the sinews of his stones are wrapped together. His bones are as strong pieces of brass; his bones are like bars of iron. He is the chief of the ways of God."

Job 40

The dawn primordial echoes the land;
Behind the thorns there hunt two creeping hands.
As exultation rushing heart to beat,
The ground beneath vibrates his shaking feet.
For here Behemoth walks in fading light,
And but for flint and flame would rule the night.
Unrushed by waters pounding icy cold,
To slaughter one of these is fear untold.
Precursor, man primeval poetry,
His spear and fear and flooding ecstasy.
Like hunting wolves they howling to the moon,
Their grunts are sonnets, soul and earth in tune.
As rushing forth to muscle, tusk and death,
By flame they drive into the killing cleft,
Where spears incise and burst a fount of death.
The breath of beast is drained from empty flesh,
Yet in this fill of blood is love's restraint;
For here the heart that kills is heart that paints.
As Sorcerer and Venus dance and spin,
Romancing early man with phoenix kin,
For in his eyes the poetry of Earth,
In which he paints the cave with all her worth.
Within the spear is fear and majesty,
Austere that balance we have cast to sea.

Poetry
Part III: The Sanitised Earth

"Lo, let that night be solitary, let no joyful voice come therein. Let them curse it that curse the day, who are ready to raise up their mourning."
Job 3: 7-8

Here in utopia and end of times,
I roamed Smithsonian in Hall of Shrines.
By Salamanders intravenous hung,
By *Sorcerer and Venus* cut and slung.
And everything bowed to science's Throne,
The word to silence quantified and thrown.
For Ziz was birthed of Babylon and air,
And Earth our sacrifice beyond repair.
As under Tower men became as one,
The Words of power all became undone.
By a tormented tusk, a fossil head,
A monument to blood that man has shed.
Here stands Behemoth to extinction sent:
No lamentation nor a flute ascent.
All his genetics cut obsidian;
No dialect to void oblivion.
And yet Leviathan had no display,
No violent end nor cage of man by day.
For us that Serpent roams in word alone;
His bones are metaphors, the stars his home.
Yet on the day chaos again is stirred,
How many shall be slayed in jaws of Word?
For when Leviathan and Pneuma form,
The violent seas shall not contain their storm.

Satan and the Rock
Part I

Out deep upon the sea in fruitless night,
Life ceaselessly flowing on empty tides,
My soul awaiting the adorning light,
Yet sun brings none when mending nets untied.

From coastal wilderness a voice distilled,
Though faith was senseless, still I gave my trust.
My boat once empty now by friendship filled:
New nets and fish to which I am now thrust.

In miracles I heard your kingdom claim,
As following in faith from crowd to storms.
Of twelve was I who first did know your name,
Yet richest praise to prideful heart reforms.

For Satan and the Rock make war in me,
Our friendship and my pride opposing seas.

Satan and the Rock
Part II

The room was full of death like candlelight;
The bread and wine your friends now enemies.
Your sorrow weighing deep upon the night:
Oh, how could I fulfill this prophecy?

In garden dark, my pride fell into sleep,
A broken vigil, flash of sword and blood.
In courtyard fear my pride I could not keep,
My loyalty now lost into the flood.

You caught my eyes, their friendship thrice denied.
Somehow no anger there, but sorrow deep.
My pride inside anguish I tried to hide.
Our friendship wrecked like boats in tidal keep

As thrice the sun did rise in coldest sea,
My nets of guilt and grief and agony.

Satan and the Rock
Part III

Upon the sea of isolation tossed,
My heart unnerved and twisted up like rope.
Somehow in resurrection I am lost,
Our friendship gave me my eternal hope.

A voice from shore like many moons before,
I leapt from bow in sweet and prideless joy.
The swell of peace within my heart at war,
As bowed before my Jesus like a boy.

Yet friendship not so easily restored,
As thrice denied "My son, do you love me?"
In eyes of judgement and forgiveness sure,
All pride now lost "My friend, yes, I love thee."

"My son, Peter, the cross shall be your end.
Where once you fell, I'll raise you up as friend."

Under the Sun
Pain and Justice

Question
Preying vulture eyes his prize,
A boy so young with dying eyes.
Black skin barely covering
His bones and belly blistering.
Weight of pain so laid on him,
How could there be an equal sin?
Where is justice? Where is joy?
And why does pain so fill this void?
How can you claim righteousness?
For death lies in your idleness.

Answer
Did you of such primal birth
Lay the foundations of the earth?
You can claim no eminence
Against eternal genesis.
Blaming me for earthly pain,
And yet your tongue did not abstain.
Cursing crying "Crucify!"
The pain you judge, you satisfy.
So the guilt of suffering
The very crown that makes you king.

Under the Sun
Flesh and Spirit

Question
Flesh and spirit are entwined;
In paradox they are designed.
For our flesh each passing day,
Disintegrating to decay.
Yet eternity is laid
Upon our hearts so heavy weighed.
Time and the eternal wage:
A war which binds us in a cage.
This division in our souls,
Does thieve our hope of being whole.

Answer
Yet it was not always so,
For time eternal once did flow.
Tree of life encircling,
Two wells there rose of deepest spring.
Evening joy and gardening,
With time a guide to blossoming.
Ancient immortality,
Our perfect free duality.
Flesh and spirit without war,
Time splashing on eternal shores.

Under the Sun
Works and Wisdom

Question
Man his own salvation be,
For goodness lives in you and me.
Lift your hands in wisdom work,
A perfect system from the murk.
Majesty will be unfurled
If we rebuild our garden world.
All our borders broken down,
And polish Eden's ancient crown.
And the world would be as one,
As daughters live in peace with sons.

Answer
Such wisdom and vanity
Vortex in man's morality.
Look at the works of the wise,
And tell me which did not demise?
Ignorance in hearts of stone,
As wisdom crushed in liars' throne.
Wisdom fades to vanity,
As she's traded in for alchemy.
All insight and memory
Are lost in death to agony.

Under the Sun
Happiness and Joy

Question
Liberty and happiness:
The liturgies that carry us.
Their pursuit the life we bring,
To happiness hosannah sing.
Staving off all tears and pain
To make this earth a soft domain.
Dreams of endless pleasuring,
No more of mother's tethering.
Paradise! Sweet paradise
Shall be the earth once sterilised.

Answer
Look at life under the sun.
All history: Still peace not won
Lost in your own odysseys,
You search for meaning without Me.
The pursuit of happiness
May dull the instantaneous
And ultimate reality
That life is painful fallacy.
Turn your face instead to joy,
Wherein the pain still peace enjoyed.

Coelacanth Revisited
Part I: Laid in the Foundations of the Earth

From perfect still to this chaotic world,
Three coastal coelacanths in stone now curled.
From surface of the deep to dryest lands,
Eternally they watch the stars expand.
Much older than the shore which they reside,
Through all epochs the three lay stratified.
So long before the sea by man patrolled,
As bone-by-bone eternal forms laid whole.
One coelacanth so delicately laid,
That scales imprint like poetry conveyed.
He swam in laying of foundations deep,
In him the secrets of creation keep.
Another backbone preserved ten in form,
Each rib a law of earthly life informs.
The third who hovered deep so long ago,
Astounding in mosaic form below.
Each groove and bump in him is history,
In an immaculate consistency.
Yet hidden deep in the Jurassic sand,
Awaiting for their gifted human hands,
Who each within their artistry could see
The majesty from deep beneath the sea.

Coelacanth Revisited
Part II: The Stone which Builds

In obtaining of stone and chosen man,
The opening of timeless truth began.
Palaeontologist: The strangest touch,
A chosen vessel wresting with his brush.
Egyptian Prince with tablets rough to file,
To Patmos exile etching deep in style.
Although the bones were laid before their birth,
Their authorship displays them to the Earth.
The artist's voice and mind were not constrained,
Yet somehow Coelacanth remains unchanged.
Palaeontology is poetry,
As authors freely write to majesty.
Without alleviation night made dawn,
For bloom not bud a rose's perfect form.
The search of nature's law is here fulfilled,
From the eternal stone the truth distilled.
Three Coelacanths as one in love now speak,
In twin voices Hebrew entwines with Greek.
The word immutable in man at home,
Each Coelacanth translated from their stone.
As hearts of man are raised to things above,
Hold fossils up in apostolic love.

www.ingramcontent.com/pod-product-compliance
Lightning Source LLC
Chambersburg PA
CBHW041309240426
43661CB00045B/1495/J